SMART BRAIN RIGHT BRAIN

Exploring Our Universe

Om KIDZ
An imprint of Om Books International

Om Kidz | Om Books International

Reprinted in 2023

Corporate & Editorial Office
A-12, Sector 64, Noida 201 301
Uttar Pradesh, India
Phone: +91 120 477 4100
Email: editorial@ombooks.com
Website: www.ombooksinternational.com

Sales Office
107, Ansari Road, Darya Ganj
New Delhi 110 002, India
Phone: +91 11 4000 9000
Email: sales@ombooks.com

Author: Shweta Sinha
Editor: Kirti Pathak
Art & Design: Anshuman Pandey, Gaurav Bhandari, Harish Arya

ISBN: 978-93-5276-834-9

Printed in India

10 9 8 7 6 5 4 3 2

CONTENTS

1. Planet Earth

Earth is our very special home in space.

We share our planet with other humans, animals and plant-life.

It is unlike any other planet we know of, because:

1. Its atmosphere has lots and lots of oxygen.
2. It has a large supply of liquid water.

Both these things are important to support living things.

DID YOU KNOW?

Earth is the only planet known to us with living things.

If you see Earth from space, it looks like a blue and white marble.

POCKET FACT

Earth appears blue because of an abundance of water and air.

The nearest object to us in space is the Moon.

The Moon goes around the Earth. It is like a little puppy that follows Earth wherever Earth goes in space.

The Moon looks big to us only because it is so close to Earth. The Moon is actually only one-fourth the size of Earth and a million times smaller than the stars.

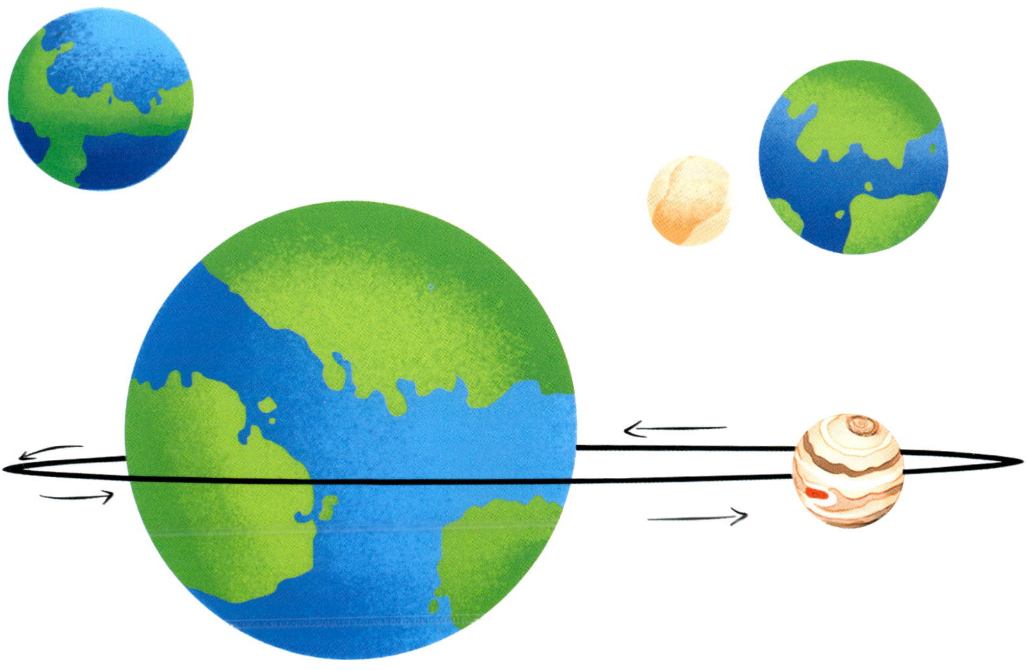

2. The Sun

The Sun gives us light and heat. The Sun also drives our weather.

Heat from the Sun warms up the air around us. It evaporates water from Earth's rivers, lakes and oceans. This is **evaporation**.

The water turns into vapour and rises up to form clouds. This is **condensation**.

The clouds then fall back upon Earth as rain, snow and hail, affecting the weather of that place. This is **precipitation**.

The Water Cycle

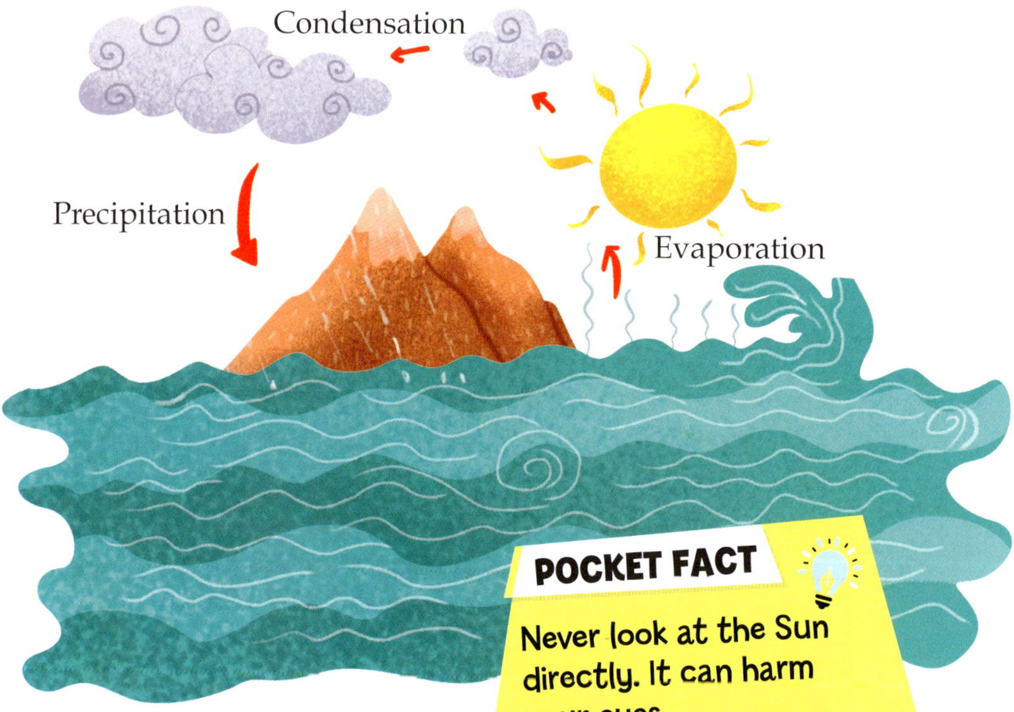

POCKET FACT

Never look at the Sun directly. It can harm your eyes.

The Sun defines our days and nights. Our day begins when the Sun rises and ends when the Sun sets.

It may seem that the Sun moves across the sky from the east to west. But, the fact is that the Sun does not move. It is our Earth that is constantly spinning like a top.

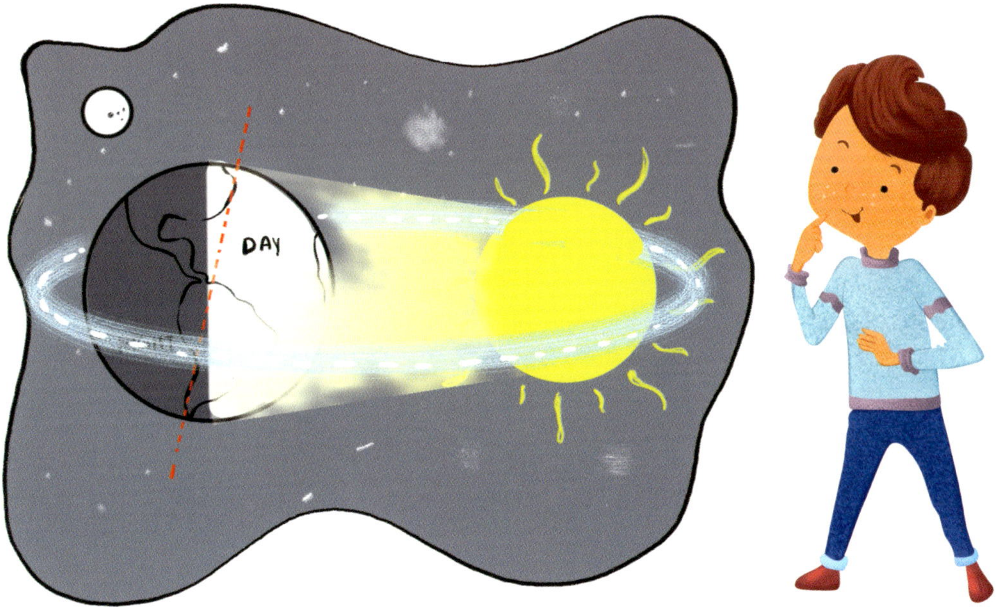

DID YOU KNOW?

The Moon does not have any light of its own. It bounces back sunlight that falls on it.

3. How Earth Moves

Days and nights

Earth is hurtling through space at breakneck speed. Its movements create day and night. Let's see how:

You need: A flashlight, a big ball or globe, a dark room.

1. Ask a friend to hold up the ball.

2. Switch off all the lights.

3. Shine the flashlight on the ball. Notice that only half the ball has light. The other half is dark.

4. Spin the ball slowly. The dark side comes into the light. And the bright side is now dark.

POCKET FACT

When Earth spins, we say it rotates. Earth makes one rotation every day.

Similarly, only half of Earth faces the Sun at any given time. That half gets sunlight and heat. We call it daytime.

The other half faces away towards space. It is cooler and darker. That is night-time.

When Earth spins, days turn into nights and nights become days.

Earth rotates around an imaginary line called the **axis**.

The axis runs from the North Pole to the South Pole.

This axis is not upright. It is slightly tilted at an angle.

In addition, Earth travels around the Sun in a circular path called an **orbit**.

It takes one year to complete one orbit.

DID YOU KNOW?

One year is 365 days long. But every four years we have a leap year which is of 366 days.

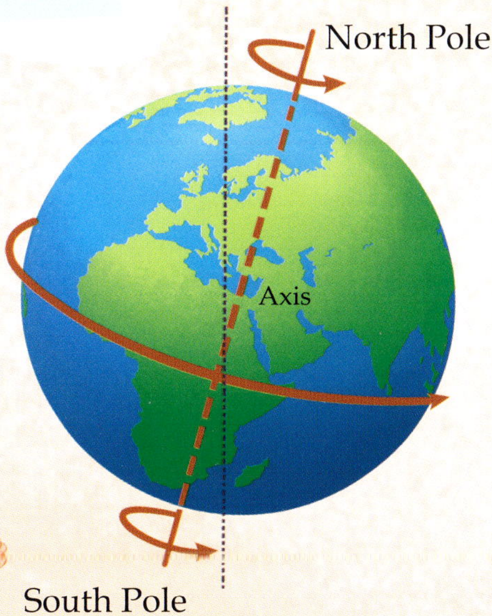

Seasons

The tilt in Earth's axis causes our annual cycle of seasons.

In June, the North Pole is tilted towards the Sun. So, the northern parts receive more sunlight and heat. This causes the summer season.

At the same time, the South Pole is tilted away from the Sun. So, the southern parts receive less sunlight and heat. This causes the cold winter season.

DID YOU KNOW?

In December, for weeks the Sun never sets in the South Pole and does not rise in the North Pole.

During December, the opposite occurs.

The South Pole tilts towards the Sun while the North Pole tilts away. As a result, it is winter in the northern parts and summer in the southern parts.

The weather conditions change every six months.

There are two other positions in Earth's orbit, when both the poles receive equal sunlight. These positions mark the spring and autumn (fall) seasons.

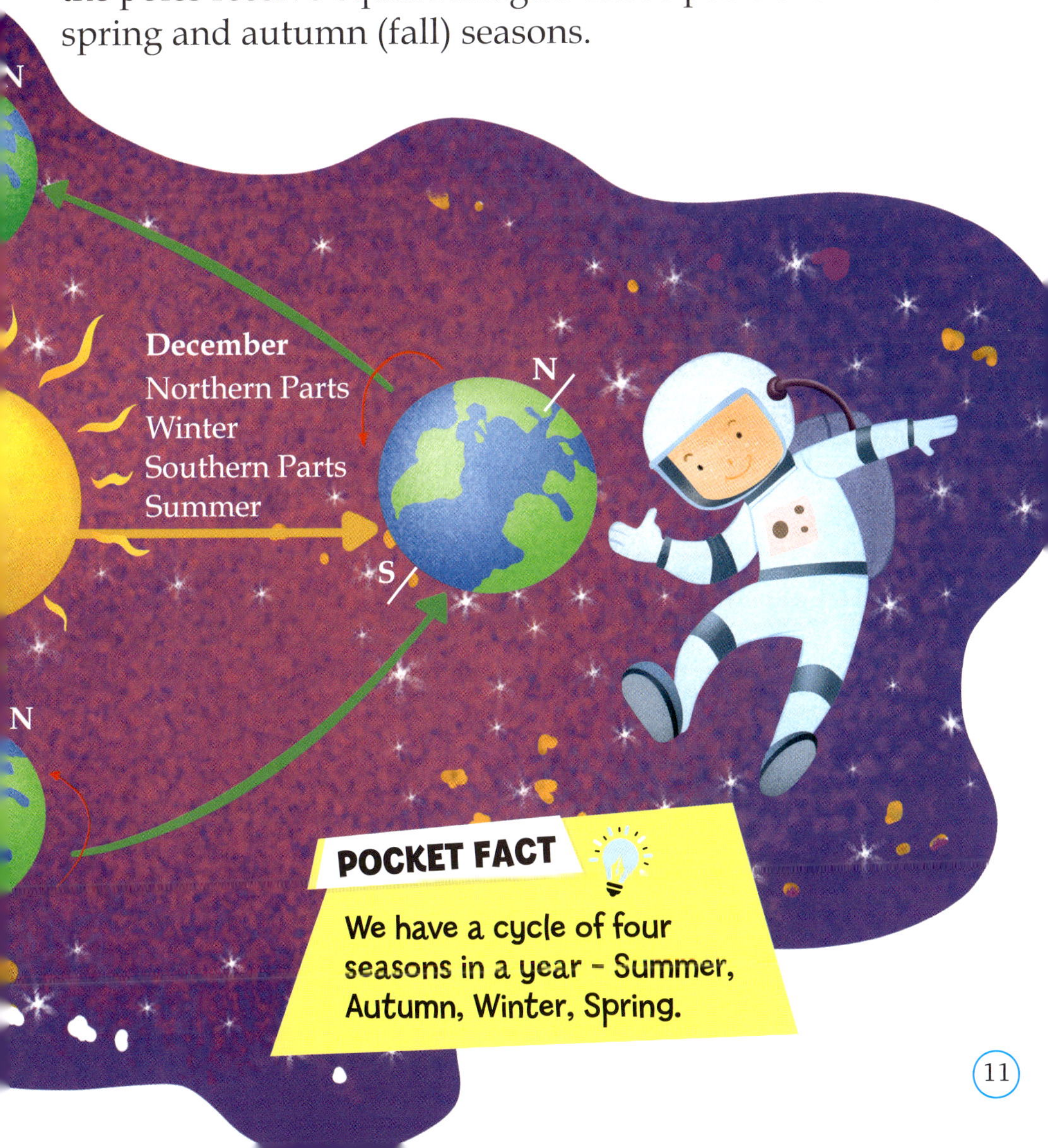

POCKET FACT

We have a cycle of four seasons in a year - Summer, Autumn, Winter, Spring.

4. The Solar System

The Sun is one of the billions of stars you see in the night sky. It is a giant ball of gases.

The Sun is so big that its gravity pulls objects in orbits around it.

The Sun and all the objects orbiting it make up the solar system.

DID YOU KNOW?

Orbits are not perfect circles. They are always oval or squashed circles.

The **solar system** includes eight planets, more than 170 moons, dwarf planets and countless asteroids and meteors.

The Sun lies at the centre of the solar system.

Our Earth is the third planet in the solar system. Sunlight takes eight minutes to travel to Earth.

Mercury: Size: 0.4 Earths Moons: 0	**Jupiter**: Size: 11 Earths Moons: 67
Venus: Size: 0.95 Earths Moons: 0	**Saturn**: Size: 9.5 Earths Moons: 62
Earth: Moons: 1	**Uranus:** Size: 4 Earths Moons: 27
Mars: Size: 0.5 Earths Moons: 2	**Neptune**: Size: 3.9 Earths Moons: 14

POCKET FACT

'Solar' is a word for all things to do with the Sun.

5. Inner Planets

Get your rockets ready and let's vroom off into space.

The first planet from the Sun is Mercury.

Mercury hides behind the Sun's brightness and is hard to see in the sky.

It is a super-hot planet with no water and almost no air.

Mercury is full of craters just like our Moon.

POCKET FACT

Mercury is hotter than an oven baking cookies.

POCKET FACT

You can see Venus in the sky just before sunrise in the east and just after sunset in the west.

Venus is the second planet in the solar system.

It is called **Earth's twin** because they both are similar in size.

Venus is the hottest planet with lots of carbon dioxide in its atmosphere.

Venus is covered with thick, yellow clouds hiding its surface.

It rains acid on Venus and there may even be fiery volcanoes.

POCKET FACT

NASA's Curiosity was the largest rover to land on Mars. It is about the size of a small SUV car.

After Venus comes Earth, and then comes Mars.

Mars looks like a red dot in the sky. It is red because it is covered with reddish dust.

Mars is too cold for liquid water. All its water is frozen at its poles.

Neither of its moons are round. They look like potatoes flying in the sky.

Mars is a fascinating place and several rovers have already been sent to learn more about it.

Mercury, Venus, Earth and Mars are called the **Inner Planets**.

They are the closest to the Sun. They are all hard and rocky.

To go to the **Outer Planets**, we need to cross the Asteroid Belt.

The Asteroid belt is filled with thousands and thousands of asteroids.

Asteroids are pieces of rock and metal. Like planets, they too orbit the Sun.

POCKET FACT

In 1801,Ceres was the first asteroid to be discovered. It is also the largest among the 6,00,000 asteroids discovered so far.

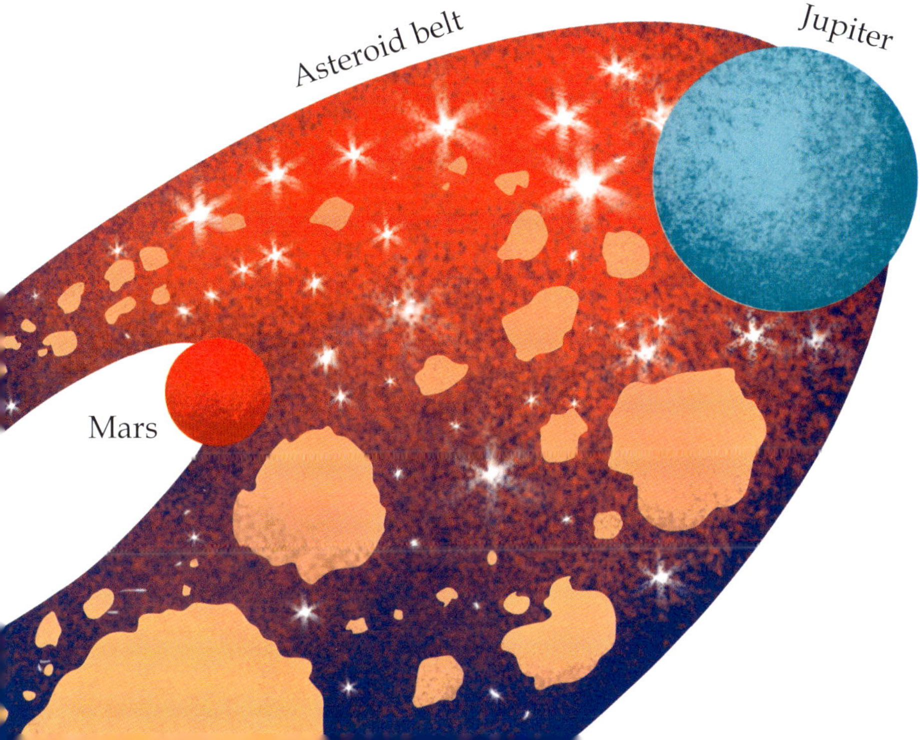

6. Outer Planets

Jupiter is the first of the Outer Planets. It is the biggest planet in our solar system.

And the heaviest too. It weighs more than all the other planets put together!

It is so big that a thousand earths can fit inside it.

Jupiter is a gas giant, with hardly any solid land.

POCKET FACT

A storm, known as the Giant Red Spot, has been raging on Jupiter for 300 years.

DID YOU KNOW?

Saturn is big, but light.
It is lighter than water.
If you could throw
Saturn into a giant
bathtub, it would float!

Saturn is the sixth planet from the Sun.

What is the most striking thing about Saturn?

You are right—its rings. There are thousands of rings around Saturn. These rings are made of ice, rock and dust.

Like Jupiter, Saturn too is a gas giant and has lots of moons.

The next planet is Uranus. Uranus is a lot like other planets

It is a gas giant like Saturn and Jupiter.

Uranus has rings like Saturn, although they are fainter.

Like Earth, it appears blue. However, Uranus gets its colour from gases such as Methane, and not from water.

But, Uranus does something that makes it stand out from the others. It rotates in a unique manner. Uranus seems to be lying on its side as it spins.

POCKET FACT

The temperature on Uranus is freezing cold because it is so far away from the Sun.

The eighth planet is Neptune.

Neptune too appears deep blue in colour.

It is the last of the outer planets.

It is four times wider than Earth and the same size as Uranus.

A year on Neptune equals 165 Earth years.

POCKET FACT

Like Jupiter, Neptune too is rather stormy with winds that blow at 2000 km/hour.

POCKET FACT

Pluto has a giant moon called Charon, which is half the size of Pluto.

We, of course, don't want to miss Pluto, our dwarf planet.

Pluto was originally thought to be the ninth planet of the solar system. But recently it was found to be smaller than even Earth's Moon. Hence, Pluto was re-labelled as a '**Dwarf Planet**'.

Pluto is so far away from the Sun that the Sun appears like another bright star in Pluto's sky.

6. Discovering Space

Over the years we have developed technologies to help us look into the depths of the universe.

The telescope was the first instrument used to stare into space. A telescope magnifies objects far away and makes them appear bigger and closer.

One of the most famous telescopes is the **Hubble Space Telescope**. The Hubble telescope is not on Earth, but in space. It is powered by sunlight and orbits Earth. Scientists control this telescope through computers. The Hubble telescope has sent us amazing images of space.

DID YOU KNOW? Telescopes were first used by people travelling in ships.

Do you know who was the first person in space?

It was Yuri Gagarin, the Russian Cosmonaut, in 1961.

And who was the first to land on the Moon?

Neil Armstrong from the USA, landed on the Moon on 20 July 1969.

The knowledge that scientists gained through telescopes made these space voyages possible. However, most space missions were unmanned. This means the spacecrafts were controlled remotely from Earth.

POCKET FACT

No one has ever travelled to another planet, but someday we may be able to live on one.

Scientists have sent several unmanned machines into space. Known as 'probes', they give us valuable information about our solar system.

In 2015, the **New Horizons** probe created history by flying past Pluto. It sent back close-up images of a heart-shaped feature on Pluto's surface.

Spirit, Opportunity and Curiosity are rovers that were sent to Mars. They are powerful robots that have helped us learn more about the planet.

As time goes by, scientists will continue to develop new technologies to further explore space.

7. Junior Astronaut

How do astronauts go off into space? They fly out in rockets.

Let's make a mini-rocket of our own.

Materials you need:

- Straws of two sizes – thin and thick
- Tape
- Crayons, markers or colour pencils
- Construction paper
- Scissors

1. Draw a rocket on paper, about 3 inches in length. Colour your rocket and cut it out.

2. Cut out about 3 inches of the thicker straw. Tape one end shut so it's completely sealed. The other straw should easily slip in and out of the thick straw.

3. Attach the thick straw to the back of your rocket with tape.

4. Slip your thin straw inside the thick straw and blow.

Watch your rocket take off in air.

Caution Make sure you point your rocket upwards when blowing so you don't blow the rocket into someone's face.

DID YOU KNOW?

The Apollo spacecrafts were designed to take astronauts to the moon and bring them back home.

Word Search

Circle the names of all the Space objects you can find in the grid below:

K	U	K	P	V	T	P	L	U	T	O
N	H	R	X	L	S	X	F	A	P	Q
E	S	H	A	U	F	L	C	Q	U	T
P	A	K	T	N	G	Z	U	K	L	K
T	T	V	I	J	U	P	I	T	E	R
U	U	F	E	L	H	S	O	A	N	E
N	R	V	T	N	M	A	R	S	O	A
E	N	R	W	M	U	U	K	I	R	R
H	U	B	B	L	E	S	H	G	B	T
M	E	R	C	U	R	Y	L	D	I	H
C	U	R	I	O	S	I	T	Y	T	C

Clues:

Curiosity
Earth
Hubble
Jupiter
Mars
Mercury
Neptune
Orbit
Pluto
Saturn
Uranus
Venus

True or False?

State whether the following statements are true or false:

1. Venus is the hottest planet in the Solar System. (True/False)

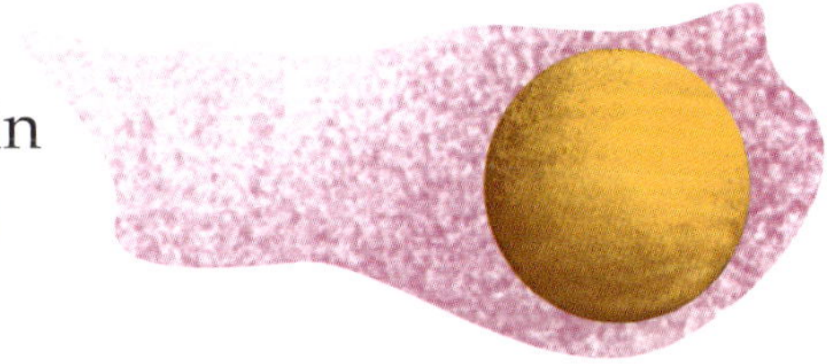

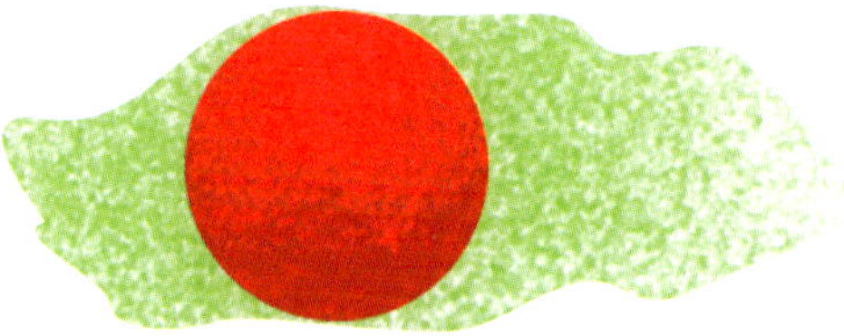

2. Mars is bigger than Earth. (True/False)

3. Uranus is the only planet to spin on its side. (True/False)

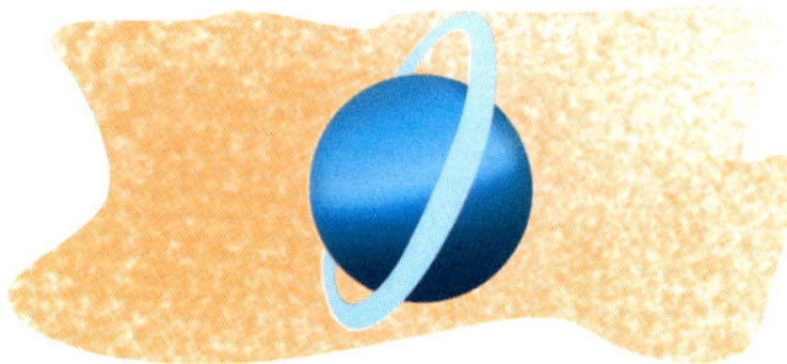

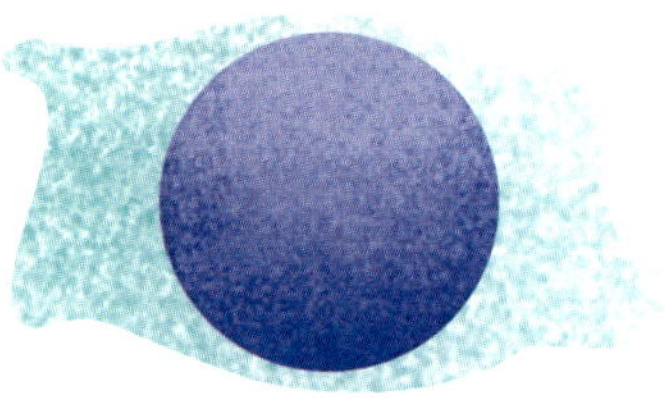

4. Neptune appears blue because it has lots of water. (True/False)

5. When the North Pole has summer, the South Pole has winter. (True/False)

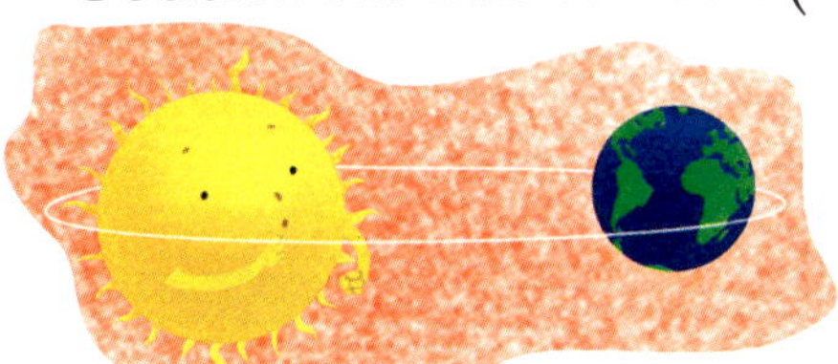

6. Days and Nights are caused by Earth's rotation. (True/False)

7. The Moon makes its own light. (True/False)

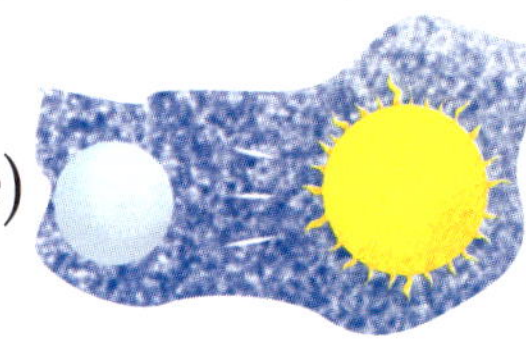

8. Curiosity was a probe sent to Pluto. (True/False)

Choose the Correct Answer:

1. How many planets are there in the solar system?

   (a) Eight (b) Six (c) Ten

2. Which planet is farthest from the Sun?

   (a) Earth (b) Neptune (c) Mars

3. Which planet has rings?

   (a) Jupiter (b) Neptune (c) Saturn

4. Light from the Sun takes _____ to reach us

   (a) 10 minutes (b) 8 minutes (c) 8 hours

5. How many days does a leap year have?

   (a) 364 (b) 365 (c) 366

6. Which planet is red in color?

   (a) Mars (b) Venus (c) Jupiter

7. What is the name of the rover that went to Mars?

   (a) Discovery (b) Challenger (c) Curiosity

8. Which planet supports living things?

   (a) Mars (b) Earth (c) Venus

Sorting out the Solar System:

Use the given clues to find out the order of the planets.

- Mercury is the planet closest to the Sun.
- Venus is next to Mercury.
- Mars is called the 'Red Planet'.
- Jupiter lies between Mars and Saturn.
- Saturn and Uranus have rings.

GLOSSARY

Asteroid	a space rock that orbits the sun
Atmosphere	the layer of gases that surround a planet or moon
Axis	the imaginary line that runs through Earth or any other object that spins around
Billion	a thousand million units
Explore	learning about new places
Gas	a wispy substance that spreads out and fills any container, like air
Gas giant	a huge planet made mostly of a ball of gas
Gravity	the force that pulls objects together. Gravity makes things fall to the ground. Gravity also makes planets keep on orbiting the Sun
Meteor	a small space rock that hits Earth's air
Orbit	the path that a planet takes around a star
Planet	objects we can see in the night sky that move in a different way than stars
Solar system	our local neighbourhood in space made up of objects that circle around the Sun
Universe	the name for the whole of space

ANSWERS

Page 28.

K	U	K	P	V	T	P	L	U	T	O
N	H	R	X	L	S	X	F	A	P	Q
E	S	H	A	U	F	L	C	Q	U	T
P	A	K	T	N	G	Z	U	K	L	K
T	T	V	I	J	U	P	I	T	E	R
U	U	F	E	L	H	S	O	A	N	E
N	R	V	T	N	M	A	R	S	O	A
E	N	R	W	M	U	U	K	I	R	R
H	U	B	B	L	E	S	H	G	B	T
M	E	R	C	U	R	Y	L	D	I	H
C	U	R	I	O	S	I	T	Y	T	C

Page 29. 1. True 2. False 3. True 4. False
5. True 6. True 7. False 8. False

Page 30. 1. (a) 2. (b) 3. (c) 4. (b)
5. (c) 6. (a) 7. (c) 8. (b)

Page 31.

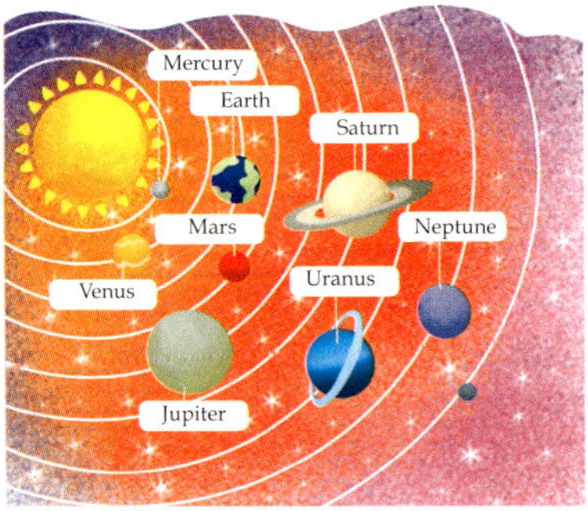